CALMING THE STORM WITHIN

Workbook
For Individuals or Groups

Published by Five Feet Twenty
PO Box 1
Lambertville, MI 48144
5feet20.com

ISBN 13: 978-0-9886137-4-4

ISBN 10: 0-9886137-4-3

Cover design by Jennifer Lassiter

Acknowledgements

I want to thank the many people who were instrumental in helping to make this project a reality.

Thank you Stu Rickert and Jim Oedy who both gave this a "test run" in the Bible studies they lead. Thanks so much for your help and input and for your friendship and support.

Rod Brandt, once again I thank you for your assistance in laying this out and giving it one final look-over for editing purposes. Your ongoing friendship, support and assistance are so appreciated.

A huge thank you goes out to Conrad Beck. Con, thank you for the hours we spent together critiquing every part of this workbook. Because of the time invested, I also need to thank Peggy, Con's wife, for giving him up during those, sometimes late, evenings. I appreciate you both more than words can say for your ongoing love, support and guidance to me and my family.

I also want to thank you, the one who holds this workbook, for your dedication to growing in your relationship with Christ and for your desire to walk in peace.

Finally, Heavenly Father, I am humbled that You have allowed me the opportunity to share what You have given me. You are truly amazing. Thank You!

Table of Contents

Welcome

Welcome to the *Calming the Storm Within Workbook* experience. I applaud you for seeking peace in your life. I pray that this study will be a true blessing to you.

This workbook was written primarily for use in a group setting, but can be just as effective, or even more so, for those who wish to use as a personal study.

I would like to offer a few hints that may be of help during this study:
- Before each session, prepare your heart for what God has in store for you;
- The page numbers referenced in the workbook match those from the printed book and will not be applicable to the e-reader or audio versions;
- The session numbers in the workbook do not always coincide with the chapters in the book because a couple of chapters are combined and one chapter is split in two different sessions.

I'm proud of you for your desire to grow closer to Jesus and to seek peace.

Blessings to you!

Jim Lange

Leader Notes/Tips

- If you have agreed to lead a group in this study, I want to commend you for your decision. I pray that this will be an incredible experience for you and will result in you and your group members finding greater peace.
- Review the questions/discussion items for each session prior to the meeting. Plan your meetings picking out the questions that are most pertinent for your group, using the secondary questions only if time permits. It is more important for the group to grow through the discussions and fellowship than going over every question.
- It is suggested that you complete several sections of the workbook prior to your first meeting so you are familiar with the format. Plan to be a session or two ahead of the group so that the material can marinate in your heart a while prior to the next session.
- Be flexible. Take things at your own pace. You may find it best to breakup some of the sessions into multiple meetings or to quit in the middle of a session and continue it at the next meeting.
- Depending on the dynamics of your group, you may want to consider combining sessions 9 and 10 into one session, as well as sessions 13 and 14.
- When asking questions of the group, be comfortable with the silence if there is not an immediate response to the questions.
- At the end of each section, participants should write down their "takeaway" from the lesson followed by an action plan. This is possibly the most important part of this study. This is where the "rubber meets the road," where change can begin to be made in your life and in the lives of those in your group. This is how this might be facilitated:
  ◇ "To wrap up today's session, let's spend a couple of minutes completing the Takeaway Action Plan and adding them to the Takeaway Summary/Action Plan in the back of the book."
  ◇ "Let's take some time sharing our takeaways along with our action plans."
- When the takeaways and action plans are discussed, you may feel led to challenge or encourage participants further by asking them questions such as:
  ◇ "Mary, what would it mean to you if you made this change in your life?"
  ◇ "Bob, how important is making this change to you?"
  ◇ "Larry, if you are serious about wanting to do this, how can we help you to accomplish this?"

- Depending on how serious the person is about making a change, you might consider discussing ways in which the group can hold them accountable. Refer to the Takeaway Summary/Action Plan at the back of the book for some suggestions on ways to do this. Remember, this is for their benefit, and as a leader by helping them to overcome their obstacles, you are showing love to that person.
- When praying the prayer at the end of each section, feel free to have one person pray this or pray it together as a group. Don't feel like you need to pray this prayer, it is there in case you would like to use it. Lead the prayer time as appropriate for your group.
- As a part of your prayer time, you can also consider using the ACTS method of prayer. (See Appendix D, which can be found at **calmingthestormwithin.com/appendix** for a summary of this.) You can encourage group members to add further expression to God through praise (Eg. "God You are awesome", "God, You are the creator of all!", etc...) and thanksgiving ("God, thank You for this group.", "Lord, thank You for my family.", "Father, thank you for what You revealed to me today.") These prayers of praise and thanksgiving can be spoken or unspoken.
- There is not a "right way" or "wrong way" to use this guide. You are encouraged to be creative in tailoring it to meet the specific needs and dynamics of your group as well as being a good fit for your personality and leadership style.
- Prayer should be an integral part of your leadership of the group. Throughout the study, be sure to ask the Lord to assist and guide you in preparing for and leading the group. Breath prayers during each session are beneficial as well: Lord, guide us; or Lord, lead us; or God, Show me if I should speak now; or Give me the words to say right now or prompt someone else to speak something helpful.

"You are the light of the world. A city on a hill cannot be hidden. Neither do people light a lamp and put it under a bowl. Instead they put it on its stand, and it gives light to everyone in the house. In the same way, let your light shine before men, that they may see your good deeds and praise your Father in heaven."
Matthew 5:14-16

Session 1

Chapter 1 (The Peace I Want)
Chapter 2 (Embrace the Chaos)

In preparation for the first session, read Chapter 1 (The Peace I Want) and Chapter 2 (Embrace the Chaos) in *Calming the Storm Within*.

Ice-breaker

Describe a time when your plans were totally upset because of circumstances outside of your control and what you were feeling at that time.

Questions for Chapter 1

Describe a time when you, or someone you know, experienced something like Horatio Spafford, the author of *It Is Well With My Soul*. How did you (or they) deal with it? Under those circumstances, how do you think it was possible for Spafford to believe in his heart that it was well with his soul?

In *Even Tough Times Are Good* (p. 7), Jim tells the stories about his daughter waking up late for her exam and him receiving word that the speaker he had lined up for the Prayer Breakfast cancelled and how these events caused much distress for them. What was most meaningful to you in these stories?

In the next section (p. 9) we learn that *Amen* actually means "So Be It." How does this change the way you think about prayer? What is it about you that might make those closest to you to say that you are a "So Be It" person? What can you do to become more of a "So Be It" person?

In *Receive or Go Get?* (p. 10), we learn that we must, both, receive and pursue peace. How might you have previously thought differently about this?

On a scale of 1 – 10 with 10 being extremely peaceful, how would you rate the level of peace in your life regardless of circumstances over this past week? How about over this past year?

Questions for Chapter 2

In the opening of this chapter, a case is built that chaos is not the opposite of peace and that chaos can actually help one become a more peaceful person. What are your thoughts about this?

"Christ Followers are Unstable" (p. 15). Explain the basis for agreeing or disagreeing with this.

In *Robert and Martial Arts* (p. 17), Jim discloses how his son typically does not like to get out of his comfort zone. In what ways can you relate to this? How do you think your life would be different if you looked for ways to get out of your comfort zone?

Our Heavenly Father will sometimes push us into pain or allow pain for our own benefit. Give some examples from your life when this has proven to be true.

In *Other Positives of Pain* (p. 18), we learn that many good things can come from our painful experiences. What are some positive things that have resulted from pain or chaos in your life?

In Jim's story about his basketball practice (p. 19), some difficult circumstances were needed to open him up to receive coaching and input from his teammates. Describe a time when you experienced some hardship which made you more willing to accept advice? In what area of your life are you least willing to receive input or correction? Why? What can you do to change that?

In *So Embrace It* (p. 22), we learn that the reason God allows chaos (pain, turmoil, trouble) in our lives is that He knows that the only place to find true peace is through Him. Hopefully, the chaos in our lives will draw us closer to Him, where we can find true peace. Explain why you agree or disagree with this.

How has your perception of trouble and chaos changed after reading this chapter? In your own words, describe how chaos can actually help you find peace?

Refer back to your response to the ice-breaker question. What did you learn, or what good has come, from that experience?

Takeaway: What is your biggest takeaway from this session?

Action Plan: What change would you like to make in your life?

Add these to the *Takeaway Summary/Action Plan* at the back of this book.

Pray this prayer together:

Heavenly Father, You are amazing! Thank You for being You, the One in control! Lord, I want peace, the peace that can only come from You. Please forgive me for allowing worry, anxiety and circumstances to steal my peace. I know that this is really a control issue on my part. So please God help me guard my heart and protect me from the enemy and help me let go of those things I want to hang on to. Help me continue to recognize You as the One in control of everything. Amen.

Session 2

Chapter 3 (Peace Stealers)

In preparation for the first session, read Chapter 3 (Peace Stealers) in *Calming the Storm Within*.

Ice-breaker

What is one of your pet-peeves, or something about others that drives you crazy? How do you feel and how do you typically react when someone does this?

Questions for Chapter 3

Jim opens this chapter by explaining how he has felt responsible for his wife's happiness and how this has created stress in him and in his relationship with his wife. He also said that he has typically defined success based upon outcomes (winning a game, high sales numbers or a happy wife). How is this true in your life? How could this thinking lead to inappropriate actions?

What is your basis for agreeing or disagreeing with the following?

A. All negative stress is rooted in control and fear.

B. It is your choice whether to be angry or not.

C. "Any lack of peace that I experience is simply because I am focusing on my issues and me rather than on Jesus."

What do we learn about the importance of focusing on Jesus in Matthew 14:25-31?

Our peace really cannot be stolen from us—when we lose our peace it is because we have chosen to give it away. How you have seen this happen in your life?

In *Other Peace Stealers* (p. 26), some common "peace stealers" are listed, those things which might cause us to give up our peace (go to calmingthestormwithin.com/appendix and review appendix C for some additional peace stealers). What are you currently allowing to steal your peace? How are these areas really a control issue for you? Is your selfishness keeping you here? If not, what is? If you are willing, declare to your group that you no longer wish to control this area of your life.

In *Give Me The Remote* (p. 29), we learn that we, as a society, like to take control:
- Holding the remote control;
- Living in a gated community;
- Having a security system on our homes;
- Building up our retirement accounts.

Taking control is not all bad but can be taken overboard, especially if it is rooted in fear. Seriously consider what things you do to take control. What is the underlying reason for desiring control (Is it because you think that no one else, even God, can do it but you?)?

It is suggested that we shift our self-talk during difficult times from, "Why is this happening to me?" to "What is God doing for me?" If you were able to make this shift, what difference do you think it would make in the level of peace in your life?

Jim shared about his difficult, gut-wrenching situation with his former boss and how that turned out to be one of the greatest blessings in his life (p. 31). Tell about how something similar has happened in your life.

Read Romans 8:28. If you truly lived as if you believed this, what would that do to your level of peace? What is keeping you from living in this manner?

The trees in Jim's yard that bent severely during an ice storm but did not break were actually stronger for the experience even though many trees in his community broke (p. 32). He used this as an illustration of our lives—if we are so desirous of control, we too could be broken. However, if we bend like his birch trees and "go with the flow" and let God have control of our lives, we too, could be restored and be stronger. How does this analogy speak to you?

In *Worry and Anxiety = Sin* (p. 33), we see that worry and anxiety are sin because they are dishonoring to God. Read Romans 14:23 and share why you agree or disagree with this statement.

Read Philippians 2:28. How does it make you feel knowing that the Apostle Paul experienced anxiety?

What are some of the negative effects of worry and anxiety in your life?

At the beginning of *What about Spiritual Warfare?* (p. 35) is this quote from CS Lewis, "There are two equal and opposite errors into which our race can fall about the devils. One is to disbelieve in their existence. The other is to believe, and to feel an excessive and unhealthy interest in them. They themselves are equally pleased by both errors, and hail a materialist or magician with the same delight." How can falling on either of the two ends of the spectrum mentioned above have a negative impact on the level of peace in your life?

Which end do you tend to lean toward?

What did Jesus model for us in Mathew 4 that can be effective for us in dealing with spiritual warfare?

On a scale from 1-10 with 1 being "very little or none" and 10 being "control freak," how would you rate your desire to control and why? How would those closest to you rate you and why? If you had a lower desire to control, what do you think would happen to the level of peace in your life?

Refer back to your response to the ice-breaker question. What type of response would be more God-honoring?

Takeaway: What is your biggest takeaway from this session?

Action Plan: What change would you like to make in your life?

Add these to the *Takeaway Summary/Action Plan* at the back of this book.

Pray this prayer together:

Heavenly Father, You are amazing! Thank You for being You, the One in control! Lord, I want peace, the peace that can only come from You. Please forgive me for allowing worry, anxiety and circumstances to steal my peace. I know that this is really a control issue on my part. So please God help me guard my heart and protect me from the enemy and help me let go of those things I want to hang on to. Help me continue to recognize You as the One in control of everything. Amen.

Session 3

Chapter 4 (The Path to Peace)

In preparation for the first session, read Chapter 4 (The Path to Peace) in *Calming the Storm Within*.

Ice-breaker

Describe a circumstance when you thought it was impossible to have peace.

Questions for Chapter 4

Chapter 4 begins with a cute story of a man who showed incredible wisdom in the way be "bargained" for peace. What do you think about the statement, "Unlike this man, we don't have to bargain to get peace. It is readily available to each of us."? Explain why you think this is true or not.

In *A False Start I am Thankful For* (p. 40), we learn that the words of the Apostle Paul in Philippians 4:4-9 were written while he was in a prison cell. The prisons in those days were nothing like our prisons today and it is possible that Paul was standing in human waste. How would it be possible for anyone to write such words under these circumstances?

On Easter morning at church, God spoke clearly to Jim about what needed to be added to this book (p. 44). Describe a time when you knew God was speaking to you. Explain why you believe or don't believe that God speaks to us personally today? In what ways can we be sure that it is God speaking to us?

In *Paul's Way to Peace* (p. 44), Paul's instructions are summarized:
- Rejoice always...regardless of your circumstances;
- Be gentle—some translations say "considerate"—with others;
- Know that God is always with you or nearby (Some scholars think this could also mean that we are to let our gentleness be known because the Lord is coming back soon.);
- Choose not to be anxious;

- Go to God in prayer, with thanksgiving, for everything...even small stuff;
- Keep your mind focused on good things...in other words, "garbage in, garbage out."

Explain which of these are easier for you to do and which are more challenging. What, if anything, did you notice about each other's responses?

After reading *The Master Plan* (p. 46), why do you think God tells us to do things that He knows we cannot do on our own?

Refer back to your response to the ice-breaker question. In what way have your thoughts changed about the possibility of finding peace in the circumstance you described?

Takeaway: What is your biggest takeaway from this session?

Action Plan: What change would you like to make in your life?

Add these to the *Takeaway Summary/Action Plan* at the back of this book.

Pray this prayer together:

Lord God, I am so thankful that You have provided a way to peace. You know my heart Lord, and you know that I desire peace. Please open my eyes to see and my heart to understand as I read the coming pages. Show me a new way Father. Please don't let me be deceived. I'm counting on You. I'm trusting You. God, lead me. Amen.

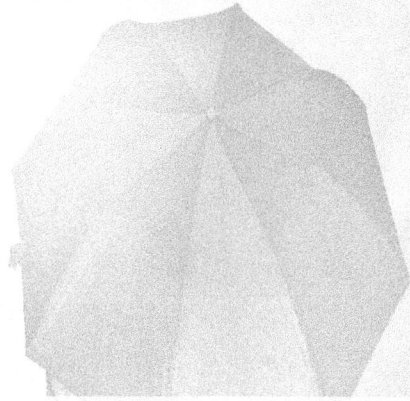

Session 4

Chapter 5 (The Only Way)

In preparation for the next session, read the first half of Chapter 5 (The Only Way) in *Calming the Storm Within* (up until *Saved From or Saved To?* – p. 59 of the hard-copy book).

Ice-breaker

What are some of the different ways that people believe that you can get into Heaven?

Questions for Chapter 5

This chapter opens with Jesus' words in John 14:6, "I am the way and the truth and the life. No one comes to the Father except through me." Explain why you think is inclusive or exclusive.

If there has been a time in your life when you hoped, like the unknown author of the poem in this chapter (p. 52), that when you died, you would be "Big enough to keep", tell about it. Whether or not you have ever felt this way, consider your current actions and tell how they might be an indication that you are trying to earn God's approval.

In telling his story, Jim discloses that as his income and net worth grew, he was surprised that the level of peace in his life diminished (p. 53). Jim was looking for peace from his bank account balance. In what ways have you looked for peace in ineffective ways?

In *Substitutionary Atonement* (p. 55), we read that the Christian faith is all about our infractions being paid by someone else (Jesus, our "scapegoat") and that we cannot pay for them on our own. What are your thoughts about that?

Have you asked God for forgiveness and for Jesus to be your Lord and Savior? If so, what questions or doubts did you have before making that commitment? If you have not made this commitment, what questions or doubts do you have?

Jim writes that he feels we often mess this up in the Church. *We tell people they can say a certain prayer and they can be "saved." (In fact, I don't see anywhere in the Bible where a "prayer" is necessary for salvation.) We focus on the "and you will be saved" part of Romans 10:9 but we forget the "Jesus is Lord" part of that same verse. If someone is your lord, you follow them and obey them. When we commit to this with Jesus, we are in essence committing to an exchange, our life for the life of Jesus* (p. 57).

- Explain your thoughts about "saying a prayer" as it relates to salvation.

- What does a *true* commitment to Jesus, recognizing Him as your **Lord**, mean to you?

  ◊ As a result of that, how is it reflected by the way you...
    ▫ Live your life?
    ▫ Work at your job?
    ▫ Speak to or relate to others?
    ▫ Act as a parent and/or as a son/daughter toward your parents?
    ▫ Treat your spouse, if married?

Many Christians claim that a life lived with Jesus is so much easier. Jim claims otherwise. He says that, *If you make this commitment it will mean that you will have some scary moments; Jesus said so. It may make you feel extremely unsafe and unsure at times. You may face pain and heartache. You may be asked by Him to do things you don't want to do* (p. 57).

- What do you think about this and how does it make you feel?

- How could this push people away from Jesus or attract them toward Him?

- How does knowing this change the way you share Jesus with someone else?

But the good news is that a life lived through Him is guaranteed to be much richer, fuller and more meaningful than a life lived without Him. Though it may feel unsteady at times, being in His arms is truly the safest place you can be, and, it brings peace, which you never thought was possible.

- How does this alleviate any fears you may have?

- Explain how this might bring a person comfort or how they might be skeptical about this.

What is holding you back from fully committing your life to Jesus and allowing Him to truly be the Lord of your life? It is encouraged that you openly discuss this with the people in your group or a trusted friend or advisor.

Refer back to your response to the ice-breaker question. How do you believe that a person enters the kingdom of Heaven?

Takeaway: What is your biggest takeaway from this session?

Action Plan: What change would you like to make in your life?

Add these to the *Takeaway Summary/Action Plan* at the back of this book.

Pray this prayer together:

Heavenly Father, I thank You that You have made a way for me to have my relationship with You restored. I am so thankful that You have made it clear to me that this is not something I can do on my own...that I cannot "earn" my way into a relationship with You. Thank You for the greatest gift of all, the gift of Your one and only Son, who died a gruesome death, all for me. Thank You for His resurrection which allows me to experience eternal life with You. Please continue to impress this upon my heart and never let me forget this wonderful gift. Thank You Lord! Amen.

Session 5

Chapter 5 (The Only Way)

In preparation for the next session, read the second half of Chapter 5 (The Only Way) in *Calming the Storm Within* (from Saved From or Saved To? – p. 59 of hard-copy book - to the end of the chapter).

Ice-breaker

Describe a time when you were so engrossed in the moment that nothing else seemed to matter. Why do you suppose this was the case?

Questions for Chapter 5

What are the indications or characteristics of a Bible-believing church?

Read Ecclesiastes 4:9-10 and Proverbs 27:17. List 1-3 good friends who you can ask to help you on your journey with Jesus. (Regardless of how long ago you committed your life to Jesus, it is still important to have others ahead of you to help guide you).

In *Saved From or Saved To?* (p. 59) that control word is brought up again and we learn that our desire to control can actually keep us from experiencing the life Jesus desires for us, life to the full. How do you see that your desire to control is limiting the fullness of your life?

In *Living in the Moment* (p. 60), Jesus' words from John 16:33 are quoted: "In this life you will have trouble." As discussed previously, following Jesus does not keep us from trouble but might actually bring us more trouble. Look at the entire verse again:

> "I have told you these things, so that in me you may have peace.
> In this world you will have trouble.
> But take heart! I have overcome the world."

- If Jesus had only promised trouble and said no more, how would that have impacted our ability to experience peace in all circumstances?

In that same section, the nine fruit of the Spirit are explored:

> But the fruit of the Spirit is love, joy, peace, patience, kindness, goodness, faithfulness, gentleness and self-control. (Galatians 5:22-23)

It seems that many times people exhibit the "fruit of their circumstances" rather than the fruit of the Spirit. Explain how this might be true for a person.

"Our main business is not to see what lies dimly at a distance, but do what clearly lies at hand."[1] (p. 62) These are the words of Thomas Carlyle.

- What does this mean to you?

- On a scale from 1-10 with 1 being "not very" to 10 being "very," how would you rate yourself in your ability to live in compartments of the moment (to shut off the past and the future, and only focus on what lies ahead of you now)?

Read Helen Mallicoat's poem:

I AM

I was regretting the past and fearing the future.
Suddenly my Lord was speaking.
"My name is I AM."
He paused. I waited. He continued,
"When you live in the past with its mistakes and
regrets, it is hard. I am not there.
My name is not I WAS.
When you live in the future, with its problems and
fears, it is hard. I am not there.

---

[1] Dale Carnegie, How to Stop Worrying And Start Living - Simon & Schuster: 1984 - p. 23-25

My name is not I WILL BE.
When you live in this moment it is not hard.
I am here,
My name is I AM.”

How does this change the way you view your regrets and worries?

In *God of Peace* (p. 63), it is mentioned that peace is attainable for anyone. Explain how you believe this is true or not in your life.

Why might it be that God is described in the Bible as the "God of peace" more than any other adjective?

If you have not made a commitment to Jesus, share what you're thinking about right now. If you have a personal relationship with Jesus, share what you feel He is showing you or teaching you now, and how He is helping you to find an increased level of peace.

Refer back to your response to the ice-breaker question. Describe the level peace you experienced in that moment? How much were you focusing on the past or the future during this time? What correlation do you see between living in the present and your level of peace?

Takeaway: What is your biggest takeaway from this session?

Action Plan: What change would you like to make in your life?

Add these to the *Takeaway Summary/Action Plan* at the back of this book.

Pray this prayer together:

Dear God, I am so thrilled and so thankful that You are the God of Peace. Thank you for sending Your Son to die for my sins and to make a way to You. I know that it is only through that sacrifice that peace is possible for me and for that I am so thankful. Lord, help me to live in the moment and help me to have life to the full. Thank you God! Amen.

Session 6

Chapter 6 (Intimacy)

In preparation for the next session, read Chapter 6 (Intimacy) in *Calming the Storm Within*.

Ice-breaker

Think about a time in which you were trying to achieve a goal, but were unable to attain it because you did not put in the time and effort needed. What kept you from doing what you needed to do?

Questions for Chapter 6

In the opening of this chapter, five levels of knowing someone are listed. Write the name of one person you know at each level followed by approximately how many people you know in that level.

1. I know who he is.   _____

2. We went to high school together.   _____

3. He/she and I are friends.   _____

4. He/she and I see each other every week and we talk often. _____

5. He/she and I are best friends.   _____

- Are there any levels with no names listed? Why?

- As you progress from level 1 to 5, what do you notice about the approximate numbers of people you know in each category? Why might this be the case?

- At which level are you in your relationship with God?

How do you agree or disagree with the comment that, "It is only through intimacy with your Heavenly Father that you can experience the peace, which transcends all understanding"?

Read the words of Jesus in John 15:1-8. What happens to those who remain in Him? What happens to those who don't?

What does your life look like when you stay connected with God and involve Him in your daily activities? What does your life look like when you don't involve God in your daily activities?

Think of your most intimate relationship on earth. Who initiated that relationship?

With God, who must move first to create an intimate relationship? Why do you think this is so?

Read John 15:4 and Galatians 5:22-23. How do these verses relate to one another?

If you were ever in a dating relationship, list some of the things you did to get to know your partner better.

"You can be efficient with your stuff, but if you want to develop a solid relationship, you must be very inefficient in that relationship." (p. 69) What does this mean in your relationship with God?

In *Hiding in the Garden* (p. 72), it says that God wants us to bring everything to Him. What parts of your life are you trying to hide from God?

Give yourself the "White Paper Test" (p. 75). If your "white paper" is not clean, what can you do to remove the obstacles in your way?

In *Acceptance* (p. 77), it is explained that if you are a Christ-follower you are fully loved and accepted by God. At what times or under what circumstances have you felt the need to earn God's love and acceptance. How did (or does) this hinder your relationship with God?

If you are willing to pay the price to have greater intimacy with God, what things could you start doing differently? Which change will you commit to?

Refer back to your response to the ice-breaker question. Are there any similarities between your response and the things that are holding you back from giving God the time and effort for a more intimate relationship?

Takeaway: What is your biggest takeaway from this session?

Action Plan: What change would you like to make in your life?

Add these to the *Takeaway Summary/Action Plan* at the back of this book.

Pray this prayer together:

Father God, thank you for Your presence and the way You are making Yourself more and more real in my life. Thank You for Your Son Jesus. I now know that I need Him if I am going to achieve peace, true peace. Jesus, please not only be resident in me, but be my President...the CEO of my life. Change my heart and put in me a desire to want to know You more intimately. I want all of You Lord! Draw me close and help me to trust fully in You... help my "White Paper" to be clean! Amen.

Session 7

Chapter 7 (Obedience)

In preparation for the next session, read Chapter 7 (Obedience) in *Calming the Storm Within.*

Ice-breaker

Describe a time when you were knowingly disobedient (to God, parents, a boss, etc...).

Questions for Chapter 7

Read Isaiah 32:17. Righteousness is obeying God and, according to Isaiah, it also produces peace, quietness and confidence. Describe how you have seen this correlation between righteousness and peace in your own life?

In this chapter we read about David and some of the sins he committed (p. 83). But we are told that David was a righteous man because he had a heart that desired to be righteous. What can you learn from David's actions?

In *Willfully Sinning = A Lack of Peace* (p. 87), we read that, "Exercising self control is vital in the level of peace we experience." Why do you agree or disagree with this?

Not praying is living a life separated from God and it is impossible to have true peace while distant from Him. Describe a time when you felt separated from God and how this affected your level of peace?

According to 1 Peter 4:7, what can help your prayer life?

How would you define *willfully sinning*? Read Isaiah 33:14 and Ephesians 2:1-2. What does willfully sinning and being disobedient bring into your life?

Read Mathew 6:33 and Proverbs 15:9. What are some practical things you can do to seek and pursue His righteousness?

This question is posed, "Would you be willing to run for president of the United States? Keep in mind the intense media scrutiny of your past." (p. 90) What could be uncovered from your past that you need to discuss with God?

In *Owner's Manual* (p. 90), we discover that truly seeking righteousness requires time with God developing your relationship with Him. He also states that time with Him will include time in His Word, our Owner's Manual. What are the biggest obstacles that keep you from spending more time with God? What one or two things will you commit to do to take a step toward removing those obstacles and taking a step closer to your Heavenly Father?

Refer back to your response to the ice-breaker question. How did your actions affect your personal peace?

Takeaway: What is your biggest takeaway from this session?

Action Plan: What change would you like to make in your life?

Add these to the *Takeaway Summary/Action Plan* at the back of this book.

Pray this prayer together:

Dear God, you are so Holy. Please examine my heart, Lord, and teach me Your ways. I want to obey You. I want to live a life of righteousness. I now know that the fruit of righteousness is peace. I know that without You and the amazing gift of Jesus' death for me, I cannot be truly righteous and therefore I cannot find true peace. So I thank you for that! I know that I cannot do this alone. I need You God. Please help me. Thank You for Your Word and Your instructions for life. Change my heart and help me desire to know and love You more. Make me a lover of Your Word. Make this a priority in my life so that I can know beyond a shadow of a doubt what obedience looks like Amen.

Session 8

Chapter 8 (The Counselor)

In preparation for the next session, read Chapter 8 (The Counselor) in *Calming the Storm Within*.

Ice-breaker

Describe a situation in which you had no support and felt helpless.

Questions for Chapter 8

In this chapter, we see that we are given the Holy Spirit upon our conversion to Christianity. Jesus explains that the Holy Spirit is given to help you; however you have a part to play. What is your understanding of the part you need to play in your relationship with the Holy Spirit according to Jesus' words in John 14?

What is the difference between Christians who have the Holy Spirit and a Spirit-filled Christian? How would you characterize yourself and why?

What advantages does a Spirit-filled Christian have over others when it comes to finding peace?

The Holy Spirit is one of the foundational keys to a life of peace. He is so meaningful in our lives that Jesus told His disciples that the Spirit would be of more help to them than Jesus Himself. How does this make you look differently at your need for a relationship with the Holy Spirit and for His help in your life?

In *Baptism of The Holy Spirit* (p. 100), we learn that once someone is a believer and submits to the Holy Spirit, He will give them power to do things they otherwise could not do. How have you experienced this in your life or how have you seen this in the life of someone else?

In *David Got It* (p. 100), we learn that King David was a great warrior who never lost a battle. His success was due to help of the Holy Spirit. David must have had great confidence because of the help of the Spirit. How would your life be different if you had the same level of confidence because you were filled with the Spirit? How would it affect your sense of peace?

In *Paul's Progression* (p. 103), the life of Paul and his progression as a Christian is examined. It is explained that this is a great reminder to those who feel that they must wait for God to finish His work in them before they can minister to anyone else. Regardless of where you are right now in your walk with Christ, what can you do to further your ministry to others?

In *Fruitfulness* (p. 106), the obvious is stated: that you know a tree is an orange tree based on the fruit growing on its branches. Refer to Galatians 5:22-23. What are some examples of this fruit that you have observed in the life of someone you know? Take some time on your own to do a self-evaluation of the fruit your life exhibits.

We also learn that we must relinquish control to the work of the Holy Spirit in order to bear this fruit in our lives. What is holding you back from relinquishing more control to the Spirit?

After reading *God's Will* (p. 108), we learn that the greatest commandment is to love God with all our heart. Explain what things in your life you have placed above loving God (your calendar and your checkbook are often good indicators of this).

Describe a situation in which you pursued your dreams instead of pursing God's will for you.

Refer back to your response to the ice-breaker question. How would this experience have been different had you been filled at a greater level with the Holy Spirit? What can you do to increase the presence and influence of the Holy Spirit in your life?

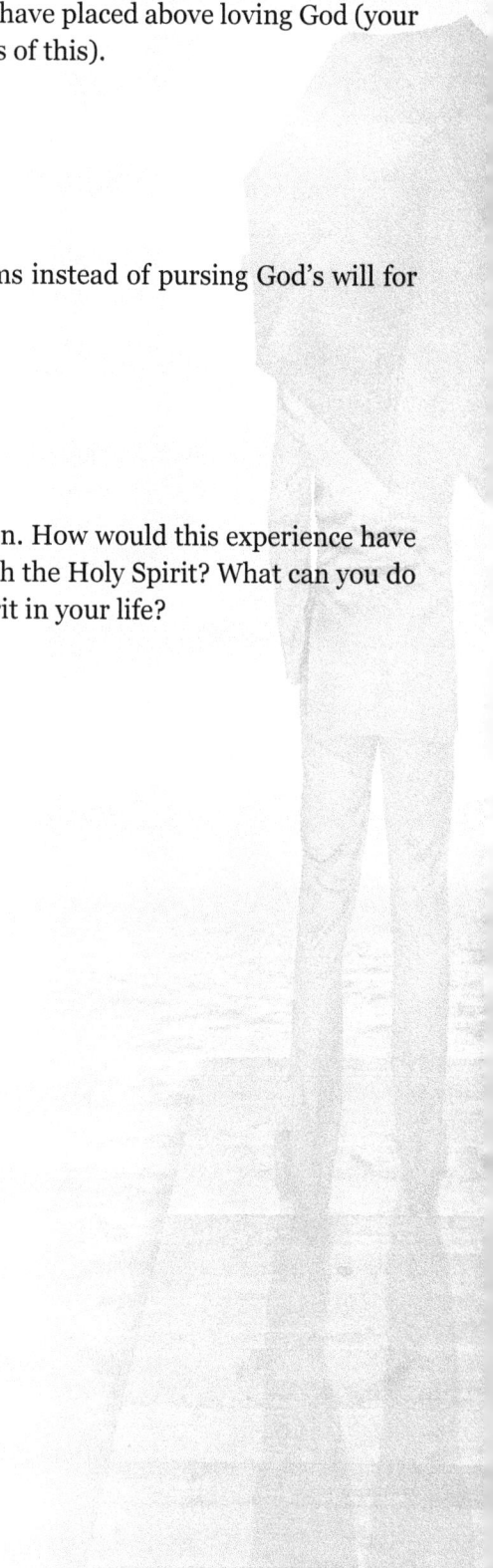

Takeaway: What is your biggest takeaway from this session?

Action Plan: What change would you like to make in your life?

Add these to the *Takeaway Summary/Action Plan* at the back of this book.

Pray this prayer together:

Father God, thank You for the gift of Your Holy Spirit. I now recognize that in order to have true peace, I must be fully submitted to the Spirit's work in my life. I deeply desire that. Please change my heart, Lord, to one that submits to Your will alone. Continually fill me with Your Spirit. Dear God, please reveal to me my part in this and give me a spirit willing to obey. Amen.

Session 9

Chapter 9 (Joy)

Note: SESSION 9 and 10 can be combined into one session if time allows.

In preparation for the next session, read Chapter 9 (Joy) in *Calming the Storm Within*. If combining the next two sessions, also read Chapter 10 (Gentleness).

Ice-breaker

List one thing that brings happiness to your life. Now list one thing that brings you much frustration or irritation in your everyday life.

Questions for Chapter 9

Read Philippians 4:4-9. What role does joy play in the level of peace in a person's life?

In this chapter, we discover that happiness is an emotion based on circumstances while joy is a quality derived from God Himself. With this in mind, think of your daily life. To what extent do external circumstances affect your level of joy? How can you be joyful even when you are unhappy?

Do you tend to be optimistic or pessimistic? Read John 15:5-11. Regardless of how God "wired" you, what actions can you take or habits can you develop to remind yourself (to renew your mind) to be joyful always?

In *Our Example* (p. 124), we are told it is our mission to find our purpose in life and then pursue it. How would understanding your purpose help you experience more joy? Consider going to calmingthestormwithin.com and downloading Jim's Discovering Your Purpose ebook (there is no charge for this). If you already know your life's purpose, share it with the group.

What are Jesus' instructions in the Great Commission (Matthew 28:18b-20)? How is fulfilling the Great Commission different for someone filled with joy versus someone who doesn't exhibit much joy?

Read 1 Thessalonians 5:16-18. Why do you think it is God's will for you to be joyful at all times?

Refer back to your response to the ice-breaker question. How can you be joyful in the midst of your everyday frustrations and irritations?

Takeaway: What is your biggest takeaway from this session?

Action Plan: What change would you like to make in your life?

Add these to the *Takeaway Summary/Action Plan* at the back of this book.

Pray this prayer together:

God, You are the author of all good things. Thank You for joy. I want more joy in my life Lord, so please help me renew my mind so that I may be transformed. Help me rejoice in You always. Help me to choose You over the worries of this life so that Your Word will be able to grow in me and I may be fruitful. Amen.

Session 10

Chapter 10 (Gentleness)

In preparation for the next session, read Chapter 10 (Gentleness) in *Calming the Storm Within*.

Ice-breaker

Describe the gentlest person you have ever met and how they made you feel.

Questions for Chapter 10

Read Philippians 4:4-9. What role does gentleness play in the level of peace in our lives?

In the beginning of this chapter, Jerry Bridges' book *The Practice of Godliness* is referenced. Review Jerry's five strategies for obeying the biblical command to be gentle. Which of these comes most naturally for you and which is most difficult?

Whether you have the "considerate" or "gentleness" gene or not, take some time right now to ask the Holy Spirit to help you develop the fruit of gentleness.

In *Humility* (p. 131), we learn that being prideful is one way to NOT be gentle and that the fall that comes with pride will not be peaceful. Read Proverbs 16:18. Where have you seen pride come before destruction, either in you or someone else? What impact do you think this had on your, or their, sense of peace?

In *Obedience* (p. 131), we see that gentleness is not just a suggestion, but a command from God and that when we are not gentle, we are disobeying Him. How does this affect your view of gentleness?

Read Proverbs 15:1. Give an example of when your gentle answer turned away wrath and another example of when your harsh word stirred up anger.

Proverbs 25:15 says *through patience a ruler can be persuaded, and a gentle tongue can break a bone.* This means that gentleness can help us accomplish difficult things. Give an example of an experience where this proved to be true for you and a time when your lack of gentleness caused difficulties.

What is it about a gentle person that makes other people want to be with them? Think about someone you like to be around and another person you don't care to be with. What is your perception of the difference in their levels of gentleness?

In *The Example of the Samaritan* (p. 133), James 4:1-2 is used to point out that it is our own selfish desires that cause fights and quarrels in our lives thus stealing our peace. What steps can you take to become more "others focused" in your life rather than self-focused?

20 years ago (or before you knew Jesus), how would you fill in the blank? "Life is Short so
_____."

How would you fill in the blank today?

Refer back to your response to the ice-breaker question. Would you like others to think about you in this way? With than in mind, what steps would you like to take to be gentler with the people in your life?

Takeaway: What is your biggest takeaway from this session?

Action Plan: What change would you like to make in your life?

Add these to the *Takeaway Summary/Action Plan* at the back of this book.

Pray this prayer together:

Abba Father, thank You for giving us such a great example of gentleness in Jesus. Lord, I want to become meeker and gentler, like Jesus. Help me be less demanding. Help me think of others more often and of myself less often. God, remove my selfish ways! Thank You Lord! Amen.

Session 11

Chapter 11 (Don't Be Anxious)

In preparation for the next session, read Chapter 11 (Don't Be Anxious) in *Calming the Storm Within*.

Ice-breaker

Describe a time in your life when you had great anxiety.

Questions for Chapter 11

Read Philippians 4:6. How is it possible to not be anxious?

This chapter begins by pointing out that we are instructed many times to "put on," "put off," "take off" and "clothe yourselves." What is our role in carrying out these instructions?

The importance of Christians needing to "exercise" their fruit (of the Spirit) is compared to the importance of a weight lifter needing to exercise to build his muscles (p. 141). Although God is all powerful, He wants to partner with us. He wants us to be an active participant in our relationship with Him. In learning to choose not to be anxious, what might you do to exercise your "self-control" muscle?

How would your life be different if you consistently chose to do your best to honor God instead of what you wanted to do?

Read 2 Corinthians 10:5. When you are feeling anxious, what are some practical things you can do to take that anxious thought captive?

When discussing Paul's command for us to not be anxious, p. 142 says: *If he wanted to be a bit more direct with us, Paul might say, "Listen. When you are anxious, you are basically telling God that you don't trust Him to handle this. So do you trust God or not?"* In the next paragraph, Jim says that, *When I'm anxious, I'm showing God by my behavior that I am going to handle this, I don't need Him and I certainly don't believe He can help me. That may be one of the most prideful things I can do and that's not good. (God opposes the proud but gives grace to the humble. 1 Peter 5:5.) In this case, I am sinning. How does viewing your anxiety as prideful and sinful change the way you think about it?*

Two scenarios are painted of you receiving some bad news, one, while with your family and, two, while with some clients (p. 143). If this was you, do you think you would re-act differently based upon who you were with? What does your answer tell you regarding your ability to exercise self-control? What does this reveal to you about the importance of self-control in choosing to not be anxious?

In *Power of Accountability* (p.144), the importance of asking others to hold you account-able is stressed. Who in your life holds you accountable to walking in a godly manner and how often do you ask them to share what they see in you? Are there people you need to ask to hold you accountable? If so, who?

In *How Can You Trust Someone You Don't Know?* (p. 146), the importance of getting to know God is stressed. This intimacy will lead to an increase in trust. As your trust level increases, your level of anxiety will naturally decrease. What are some things you can do to get to know God better?

Read the story shared in *Take the Plunge and Prime the Pump* (p. 147). What does your decision to drink the water or prime the pump say about your level of faith?

In *The Sower* (p. 148), we learn that Jesus says that worry can actually choke God's word, making it unfruitful. Describe a time in your life when worry and anxiety kept God's word from bearing fruit in your life?

Read *Two Responses* (p. 149). What appropriate action can you take that would bring hope into a situation you are worrying about now?

In *Buckeye Fever – We Have Won* (p. 153), Jim tells a story about how knowing the outcome relieved his anxiety. What is your eternal outcome? If you are unsure, please share this with your group. (Be courageous and share as this will impact your eternity and the discussion could bless others as well) How does knowing that you have already won help you with your level of anxiety?

In *He Will NEVER Leave You nor Forsake You* (p. 154), an emotional story is told by Thomas Ramundo. How do you suppose Thomas is able to have such peace about this today? How will this story help you in your battle with anxiety?

Refer back to your response to the ice-breaker question. What could you have done differently in that situation to choose to not be anxious? With the passing of time how do you see that circumstance differently? If possible, explain how you've seen God use that situation for good.

Takeaway: What is your biggest takeaway from this session?

Action Plan: What change would you like to make in your life?

Add these to the *Takeaway Summary/Action Plan* at the back of this book.

Pray this prayer together:

Lord God, thank You for being so perfect! Father, I don't want to be anxious anymore. Please help me to simply choose not to be anxious from this point forward. Help me "prime the pump" and increase my faith in You. Help me see the big picture and understand that from an eternal perspective, my problems are so insignificant. Bring others into my life to help me keep my focus on You and to help me in the area of self-control. Help me remember that we truly have already won! Remind me often of Your promise that You will never leave me nor forsake me. Lord, I choose peace instead of anxiety and worry! Amen.

Session 12

Chapter 12 (Prayer)

In preparation for the next session, read Chapter 12 (Prayer) in *Calming the Storm Within*.

Ice-breaker

Tell about a time in your childhood when you didn't get what you wanted and how that made you feel.

Questions for Chapter 12

Read Philippians 4:4-9. What role can prayer play in the level of peace in our lives?

What does it reveal to God about you when you manipulate your prayers (like the man at the beginning of the chapter who bought the coffee cake)?

In this chapter, we are shown that God wants us to ask Him for anything and everything. However, God knows what is best for us and gives us what He deems appropriate for us. He does this in His time, not ours. Share about a time when you were waiting on God to answer a prayer and your feelings of having to wait. What are some possible reasons God may not have answered the way that you wanted?

In *Why Pray?* (p. 161), we see that God has chosen to work and partner with people on the earth to do His work. Rather than just doing it all by Himself, God has decided to delegate. What does this require of us?

Elijah shows us the most effective way to pray, to pray what God wants (p. 162). Read Matthew 6:9-13. How is this prayer of Jesus similar to that of Elijah's? How does this change your view of prayer?

We are told to pray with thanksgiving (p. 163). Why do you suppose this is important to God? What are some practical ways in which you can be more thankful?

What does Matthew 6:5-8 say about prayer? How does this change the way you feel when others pray eloquent prayers after you prayed a "less impressive" prayer?

Give an example of something you think is too small or not important enough to pray for?

Share a time when you may have prayed like the little girl described in *Pray Expectantly* (p. 167), expecting God to remove her peas?

What are your BHAGGs (Big Hairy Audacious God-sized Goals – p. 169)? How will you make praying for these a regular part of your life?

In *Pray Continually* (p. 171), we are reminded that God wants us connecting with Him and praying continually. What triggers can you use in your everyday routine to help you to pray continually?

What can hinder your prayers from being heard? How can you keep your prayers from being hindered?

In *Be Real* (p. 173), we see that prayer is nothing more than bringing what is on our mind to God, even the stuff that is causing us to lose our peace. God wants to carry our burdens, but we have to trust in Him to do so. Describe a time that you prayed about a situation and were able to turn it over to God and let him handle it? Describe the level of peace you experienced.

How does the story at the end of the chapter about Mike's experience (p. 176) encourage you in your prayer life?

We can pray with thanksgiving, pray simply, pray persistently, pray expectantly, pray small, pray big, and pray continually. In what ways does this realization change the way you will pray?

Refer back to your response to the ice-breaker question. How did not receiving what you wanted turn out to be good for you?

Takeaway: What is your biggest takeaway from this session?

Action Plan: What change would you like to make in your life?

Add these to the *Takeaway Summary/Action Plan* at the back of this book.

Pray this prayer together:

Father, You are so awesome. I am so thankful that You have made a way for me to communicate directly with You! Please Lord, help me do so more often! Help me to love prayer and hate sin. Help me to be thinking about You all the time so that I can come to You about anything, anytime (simply, continually, small, big). Help me to pray persistently and expectantly. And please reveal to me anything that might be hindering my prayers. Amen.

Session 13

Chapter 13 (Focus on the Good)

Note: SESSION 13 and 14 can be combined into one session if time allows.

In preparation for the next session, read Chapter 13 (Focus on the Good) in *Calming the Storm Within*. If combining the next two sessions, also read Chapter 14 (Prayerful Planning).

Ice-breaker

What were the best thing and the worst thing that happened to you this week?

Questions for Chapter 13

Read Philippians 4:4-9. How might focusing on the good impact the level of peace in a person's life?

Describe a time in your life when you were paying attention to the dot, or the problem, rather than all the good in the situation. How long ago was that? Looking at the situation now, describe the good that came from it.

Read Romans 8:28. If you really believed this in your heart, how would this change how you viewed problems in your life? What do you think might be holding you back from truly believing the promise in this verse?

In *But Dad!* (p. 182), Jim speaks of a time when his son complained about some difficult work. In what ways do you see yourself in this story? Read Philippians 2:14 and share your thoughts about it.

In *The Tough Boss* (p. 184), Jim explains how he used Scripture as a "weapon" to fight off evil. What in your life is "stealing" your peace (remember from chapter 3 that our peace cannot be stolen but that we sometimes choose to let go of it)? Read Ephesians 6:17. What would be a good verse(s) for you to use as a weapon in your fight for peace?

In *Me, Myself and I* (p. 185), it is mentioned that selfishness is often the cause of our "dot-watching." In the situation you described when you admitted to watching the dot (problem), explain the role selfishness played in focusing on the issue rather than the positives.

Read Romans 12:2 and Philippians 4:8. In your own words, explain how the instructions found in these verses work together to help bring peace.

Refer back to your response to the ice-breaker question. Brainstorm on some possible ways in which the negative thing from your week can become a positive in your life? What might be some practical ways to remind yourself to have a more positive outlook when you encounter future negative situations?

Takeaway: What is your biggest takeaway from this session?

Action Plan: What change would you like to make in your life?

Add these to the *Takeaway Summary/Action Plan* at the back of this book.

Pray this prayer together:

Father, You are so cool! Thank You for Your creation—there is so much good all around me! Help me focus on that goodness, on the positive stuff rather than the "dot" or the problems. I know that dots will be all around but I also know that the good stuff You have blessed me with is so much greater than my problems. Help me focus on the truly important things in my life. Especially help me to focus more on You so that You can reveal to me what is important to You. Amen.

Session 14

Chapter 14 (Prayerful Planning)

In preparation for the next session, read Chapter 14 (Prayerful Planning) in *Calming the Storm Within*.

Ice-breaker

Share a time when you were clearly not ready or prepared for something or it came upon you faster than you thought it would. How did you feel while it was happening?

Questions for Chapter 14

Describe how you think God views the planning that we do.

What is the key to effective planning?

Read *Joshua the Planner* (p. 195). Had Joshua not planned, how might the outcome have been different?

God told Joshua to attack but did not give him the details on how to attack. It's possible that God wants us to plan out the details to achieve His plan for us. What plans do you need to be making?

Jim tells a story about being late for a lunch appointment because of poor planning (p. 197). How can you relate to this story and the level of peace you experience during such times?

In *Preparation* (p. 198), Jim explains how his wife's expert planning for trips helps to make it more peaceful for the entire family. Contrast this with Jim's friend from earlier in the chapter who refused to plan for his move until three days before and had to frantically call everyone he knew for help. Clearly, poor planning can negatively affect more than just our own peace. What have you learned about preparation from this section of the book?

In *So How Can I Do This?* (p. 199), Jim gives some details about a time in his life when simply writing thoughts down on pieces of paper and organizing them in a certain way helped to bring great clarity and peace to him (a plan of sorts). Tell about a time when writing some things down helped to bring you peace, clarity or hope. How might you use this process, or something similar, in your life right now?

Read Exodus 18:13-23. Who in your life is a Jethro to you...who can help you come up with a plan in difficult times? If you can't think of anyone, ask God to bring some people to mind and write their names down, and then prayerfully consider asking them to fill this role. Who are you a Jethro to?

Jim discloses his daily, weekly, monthly and annual plan to connect with God and that he is continually looking for ways to grow closer (p. 202). Explain what you do to connect with God regularly? What could you do to improve your plan for connecting with the Lord?

Planning is not just for the big stuff in our lives. It is important in every area of our lives including money, time, sleep, recreational activities, etc. In what area of your life do you need to plan better and how could that help you to experience more peace?

Refer back to your response to the ice-breaker question. Describe the amount of planning that went into your situation and how a more detailed plan might have helped your level of peace.

Takeaway: What is your biggest takeaway from this session?

Action Plan: What change would you like to make in your life?

Add these to the *Takeaway Summary/Action Plan* at the back of this book.

Pray this prayer together:

Lord, You are a God of order and I am thankful for that. Lord, I want more order in my life. Please guide me and give me the self-control to take the time to plan with You, even if I don't want to. Help me see the incredible benefits that can come from this. Help me acknowledge You in all my ways so You can make my paths straight. Thank You Lord! Amen.

Session 15

Chapter 15 (Peace is Yours)

In preparation for the next session, read Chapter 15 (Peace is Yours) in *Calming the Storm Within*.

Ice-breaker

Share about a time when you were delayed in a car, plane or train for a long period of time. Did you know the reason for the delay? How did this knowledge, or lack of knowledge, affect your level of anxiety?

Questions for Chapter 15

What has been a difficult part of following Jesus for you? When you committed your life to Christ, to what extent were you made aware of any difficulties you might experience? How was this helpful or how may it have been helpful to you in handling difficulties?

Read John 14:2; John 14:28-31; John 16:5-6; John 16:16; John 16:20. What warning is Jesus giving His disciples? What hope is He sharing?

Read John 15:18-19; John 15:20-21; John 16:2; Luke 6:22. What is Jesus warning His followers in these verses?

Read John 16:33b. What is the primary warning in this verse?

Why would Jesus warn His disciples (and us) of these things? Explain how these warnings might help us to experience greater peace.

In *The Danger of Our Comfort Zones* (p. 212), what are the two things that we start to experience as we begin to receive God's healing from the things that bind us? How have you experienced this in your life?

Read Matthew 14:22-31 and Mark 10:17-31. Where was the safest and most comfortable place for Peter? Where was the best place for Peter and why?

Read Mark 10:17-31. By staying in his comfort zone, what impact do you think this might have had on the rich young man's level of peace and why?

Read John 16:33 again. In your own words, write an outline of all that Jesus is telling us in this verse.

Read Isaiah 28:16; Ephesians 2:19-20; Matthew 7:26-27; Psalm 118:22; Colossians 1:17. What is the significance of the truths found in these verses as it relates to peace in our lives?

Read Psalm 119:11. How can hiding God's word in your heart help you to be more peaceful in all circumstances?

"God, I'm all in. I don't care about my circumstances. Use me as you want." How would making this declaration impact the level of peace in your life? What is keeping you from making this commitment to God? Will you be courageous enough right now to ask your group, or another trusted person, to help you in this? If so, take action now.

Takeaway: What is your biggest takeaway from this session?

Action Plan: What change would you like to make in your life?

Add these to the *Takeaway Summary/Action Plan* at the back of this book.

Pray this prayer together:

Father, You are beyond words. I love You so much and I thank You for loving me like You do. I thank You for providing a way to peace. I can see that Jesus is the only way to find that peace, the peace, which surpasses all understanding. And Lord, that's what I want...that's what I am seeking right now. Please forgive me for the times that I have stayed in my comfort zone. Help me, and even challenge me, to break out of that place that I think is safe. Help me to see that it is only outside of my comfort zone where Jesus is. Help me to be like Peter and step out of the boat into the arms of Jesus so I can take hold of the peace, which He has brought me. Finally God, help me to imprint Your words on my heart so that I can have Your peace in me the rest of my days. Amen.

Takeaway Summary / Action Plan

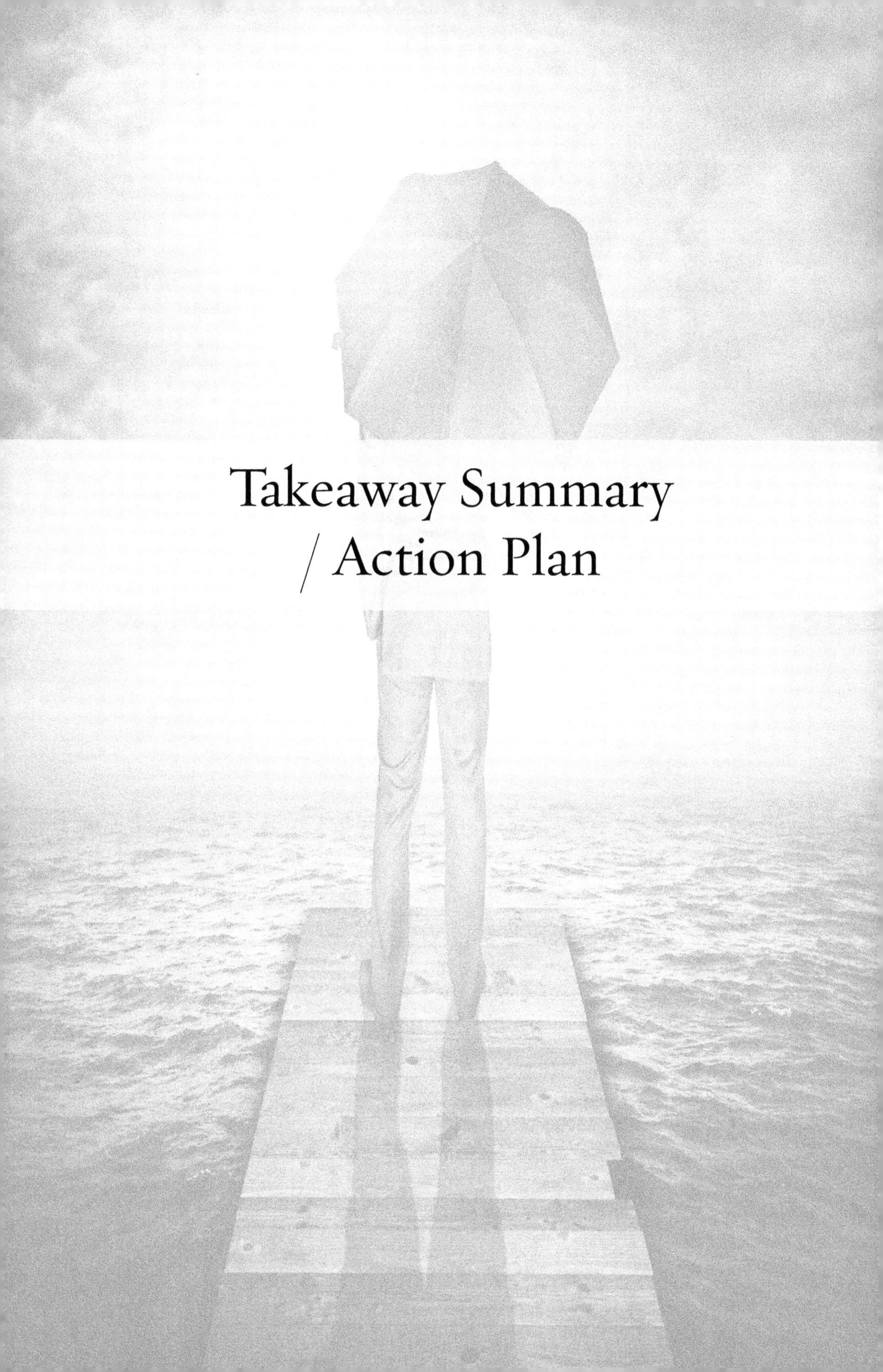

Takeaway Summary / Action Plan

Write your takeaway and the change you desire to make for each session below.

Session 1

Takeaway _____

Change I desire _____

Session 2

Takeaway _____

Change I desire _____

Session 3

Takeaway _____

Change I desire _____

Session 4

Takeaway _____

Change I desire _____

Session 5

Takeaway _____

Change I desire _____

Session 6

Takeaway _____

Change I desire _____

Session 7

Takeaway _____

Change I desire _____

Session 8

Takeaway _____

Change I desire _____

Session 9

Takeaway _____

Change I desire _____

Session 10

Takeaway _____

Change I desire _____

Session 11

Takeaway _____

Change I desire _____

Session 12

Takeaway _____

Change I desire _____

Session 13

Takeaway _____

Change I desire _____

Session 14

Takeaway _____

Change I desire _____

Session 15

Takeaway _____

Change I desire _____

There is a tendency to complete a Bible study and say, "That was nice," place the book on the shelf and not think about, or apply, what was learned again. This Takeaway Summary/Action Plan will help you to more efficiently apply, in very practical ways, what you have learned.

Take 5-10 minutes to review and pray over your 15 takeaways. Below, write the three that you feel are the highest priority for you and indicate what you commit to do and when you commit to do them. Begin right now to put your personalized plan in place to find a greater level of peace in your life.

If you have not made a commitment to follow Jesus, please consider reviewing Session 4 and 5 and talking with a trusted mentor or friend about this before proceeding. This is an essential foundation that you must have if you would like to experience true peace.

If you are following, or desire to follow, Jesus, it is encouraged that you review Session 6 before proceeding. Intimacy with Jesus is, perhaps, the most important ingredient in living a life of peace. Consider including this as one of your priority application points.

Priority Application Points

1. _____

2. _____

3. _____

Now decide who you will ask to hold you accountable and how they will do that...

I will share my priority application points with _____ and ask them to hold me accountable. I give them permission to hold me accountable by _____

_____

_____

_____

Here are some examples of how someone might be held accountable:
- Calling to check-in daily or weekly;
- Emailing daily;
- Paying a penalty when you don't get done what you commit to do. Some examples of penalties could be a donation to your church, washing another member's car, service hours at a local homeless shelter, etc...;
- Receiving a reward for doing what you say you will do. Some possible rewards could be a special night out, a day at the spa, sleeping in one day, etc...;
- Or whatever works for you.

Congratulations! I commend you for your perseverance in completing this study, for your passion to grow in your relationship with Christ and for your desire to walk in peace.

May the peace of Christ rule in your hearts, since as members of one body you were called to peace (see Colossians 3:15).

Many blessings to you!

PS. If this was a blessing to you, please consider leaving a review at this workbook's page at Amazon.com. Thank you so much!

If you would like some free resources to help you even further in your quest for peace, I invite you to visit calmingthestormwithin.com. You can also find some other encouraging resources at 5feet20.com.

Appendix - Free Resources

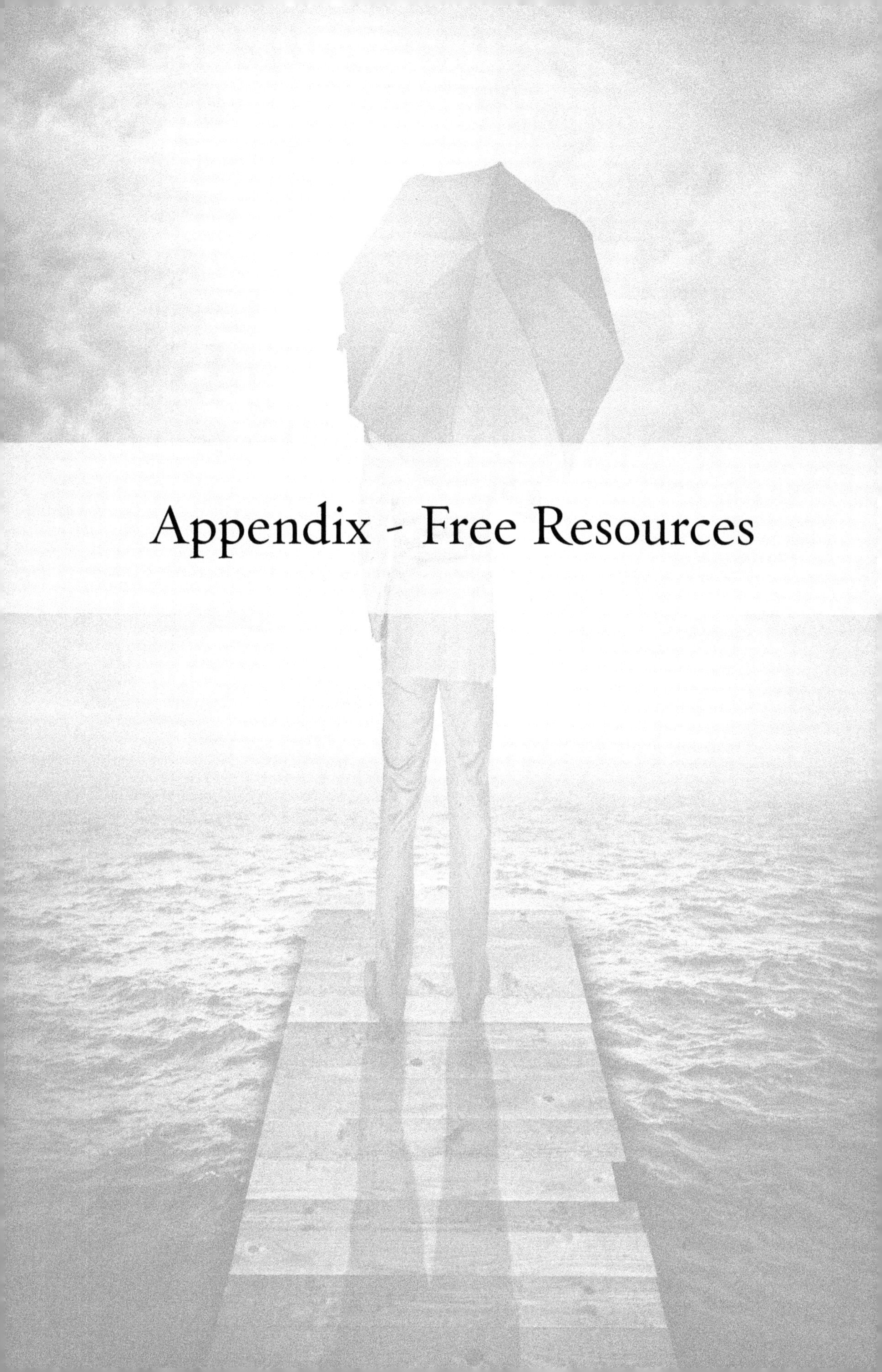

Free Resources

Here are a few things that you might find helpful:

- The Online Appendix for Calming the Storm Within (including Other Peace Stealers, Prayer Formats and The House of Peace diagram) can be found at: calmingthestormwithin.com/appendix.

- For more information and resources about finding peace: calmingthestormwithin.com/peace.

- If you'd like more information and resources regarding intimacy with God: calmingthestormwithin.com/intimacy.

- To download my Life Planning Assistant: calmingthestormwithin.com/lifeplanningassistant.

- To download my free eBook to help you discover your purpose: calmingthestormwithin.com/purpose.

- For my mom's peanut butter cake recipe: calmingthestormwithin.com/moms-peanut-butter-cake.

- To receive Jim's monthly eight-page magazine for free: 5feet20.com.

VISIT CALMINGTHESTORMWITHIN.COM TO SEE AND HEAR STORIES OF OTHERS WHO HAVE FOUND PEACE IN THE MIDST OF CHAOS.

ARE YOU A DOCTOR OR BUSINESS OWNER?

Would you like a monthly resource to give to your patients/employees/staff/clients that:

- Encourages them?
- Inspires them?
- Makes them laugh?
- Allows you to minister to them in an easy and non-threatening way?
- Helps them to grow personally and spiritually?
- Contains no advertisements?
- Is customized for your office, which also makes it a great marketing piece?

If you would like to receive a free sample of this 8-page magazine for you to evaluate, go to 5feet20.com/magazine and let me know and I will send it to you right away.

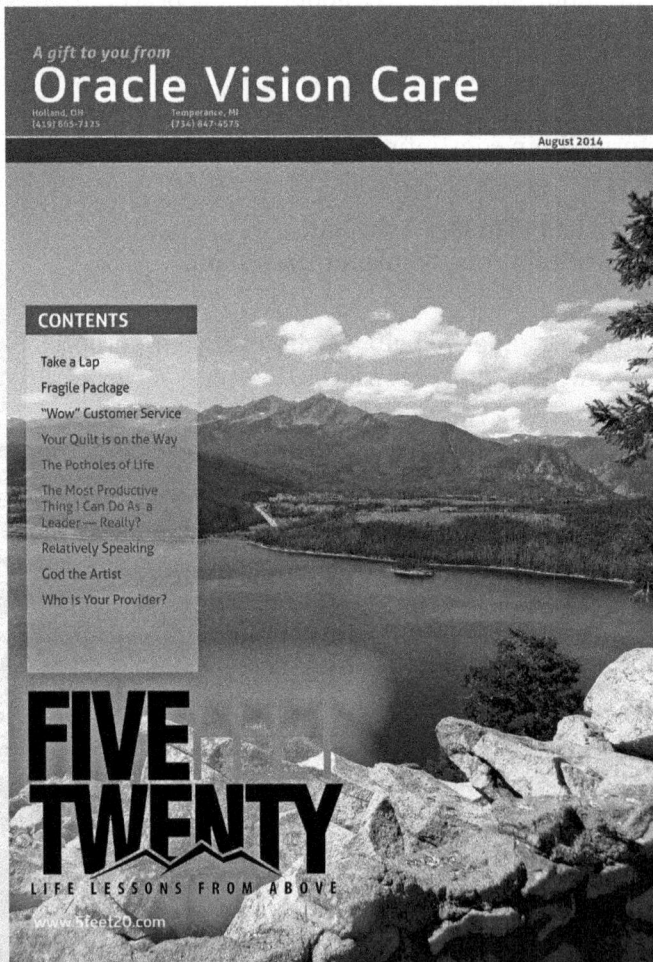

www.ingramcontent.com/pod-product-compliance
Lightning Source LLC
Chambersburg PA
CBHW062106090426

42741CB00015B/3339